The One-Year

Start your Career without !

2nd Editic

By: Mason Aksamit

This book is dedicated to the 44.2 Million Americans who did not know an alternative option, and had to pay for college through student loans. I hope this book can help your children, graduate without student loan debt.

Table of Contents:

Checklist for Finishing Your Degree Fast

Getting through college in one year is within your capabilities, even easy. To repeat, this is not a difficult thing to accomplish. There are only 3 reasons why this would be difficult:

1. You are negative to your core. One thing that you have to do when attempting to graduate quickly is to STAY POSITIVE. You will not pass every test you take. Get used to that fact. Some information will not make sense in your head as well as it does for others. For example, I am much better in history and math. I'm good at memorizing facts and analyzing numbers. That being said, I am not nearly as good at English and Science because they bore me. So avoid testing out of those courses, which are problematic for you as much as possible. My RPR (retake pass rate) was at 100%; this is because I zeroed in on the information I was missing and then I went over that specific material a second time and passed. This was probably the most helpful element of learning the material. Study, Repeat, and study again.

2. You are lazy. If you do not want to commit 20 hours a week to this, do not attempt. You will waste your money. 20 hours is not a lot of time per week, in fact at a part time job you are working more hours than you would be studying. The other thing too is that you do not have to commit to 20 hours EVERY week; you can decide to take weeks off from time to time. For me, I actually took numerous weeks off to focus more on friends, going to the gym and even spending time vacationing. In addition to taking time off, I also worked at a part time marketing job with a local martial arts school. You have the time, admit it. If you don't think you do map out your schedule at which point you will be surprised at exactly how much time is wasted daily. In addition, the best

thing about studying too, is that you can even learn while driving in the car with audio books.

3. You listen to other people's opinions of you too much. This is a huge problem with America as a whole. We care too much about how our words affect other people ensuring we are catering to others rather than actually getting something done. Get that thought out of your head immediately. You will only find unhappiness in doing so. Throughout this process, I only received support from a couple people. Friends thought my plan absurd and gave me no chance of succeeding. I learned over time to train myself to ignore them and found out I was constantly proving them wrong. I finished a Bachelor's in one year and five months and am now starting my life while they all sit in a college dorm, eating rubbish cafeteria food. And paying a fortune for the opportunity.

There is no doubt in my mind that anybody can do this. No matter what your educational background is, no matter where you grew up, where you live, race, sex, etc. You can do it, easily. Just follow my step by step program. I have created a checklist for you to use and chapters explaining each piece in detail for you to understand the plan. This checklist was developed by me after some trial and error, and then finally an eventual understanding of how the college systems work.

The following is a simple step by step checklist on how to complete your degree program fast. If you do these simple steps, I guarantee that you will complete your degree in a timely manner.

Checklist for Graduating in a Year:

Do these steps in the order that follows:

Step 1: Research Colleges/Universities ☐

Step #2: Locate each College's policies on CLEP, DSST, and Straighterline courses. ☐

Step #3: Discovering what the best program is for you to transfer your credits. ☐

Step #4: Request a "Program Evaluation" in which you see the required classes needed to get your degree and write down every type of class you need. ☐

Step #5: Explore the CLEP, DSST, and Straighterline websites to see what courses they offer that apply to the accepted exams and the Program Evaluation you are trying to complete. ☐

Step #6: Create a checklist of the tests that you will need, to obtain the classes required by your school, and order them least difficult to most difficult. ⊓

Step #7: Apply to the school that works best for your degree program. (online is probably preferred because not only is it cheaper, but it is far less time consuming) ⊓

Step #8: Start working on your tests (even before you are accepted to any of your universities) ⊓

Step #9:Be willing to mold and change your checklist of courses as you go. ⊓

Step #10: Take every test you can, until you are out of options.

⊓

Step #11: Graduate college, without student loans and in no time at all. ⊓

How do Colleges Work?

Something to make clear before you start is how the credit hour system works. For a Bachelor's degree you customarily need 120 credit hours to graduate. Now this does not mean that you have to spend 120 hours in class to get a diploma. The number comes from the average number of hours you spend each week in a class per semester. In other words, a 3 credit hour class is one that you would attend, 3 times a week for an hour for 4 months. Then when you pass the examination at the end, the 3 credit hours for that course goes towards your degree. So the average college course is 3 credit hours, implying you will have to complete 40 total classes worth 3 credit hours to graduate.

How much does school cost? Now this is a tricky question because it varies from person to person based on whether they are in state, out of state, online, community college, etc. This method will teach you how to virtually remove all of your debt and possibly not create it in the first place. So I will throw some numbers at you to commence the journey of how to graduate:

I. According to Student Loan Hero, in the United States today there is $1.45 trillion of student loan debt; that number written out looks like this: $1,450,000,000,000.

II. 43.3 million Americans live with student loan debt currently. Out of 318.9 million U.S citizens in total 242,470,820 are adults. And of those 40.4% of them graduate equaling about 97,958,211 U.S adult citizens have earned a college degree. After you do some math you will discover that 44.2% of U.S adults with a college degree have student loan debt (this includes any male or female over the age of 18, so older people who have paid their debts off don't count).

III. The average monthly student loan payment for people between the ages of 20 and 30 is $351.

IV. The average amount of debt for a student graduating college is $29,000.

So, why were all these number thrown at you? To identify a huge problem that most people are aware exists but truly do nothing about it. The average cost for a student studying at a public institution in-state is $9,410 ($37,640 for a bachelor's degree), at an out of state public school you pay $23,893 per year ($95,572 for a bachelor's degree), at a private college you pay $32,405 a year ($129,620 for a bachelor's degree). How much money you want to spend then is a direct function of where you want to attend college and how you want to attend college.

Now with the method I will teach you in the following pages you won't spend $37,640-$129,620 for a college degree. You won't even spend half of that. You will actually spend less than $15,000 for your full bachelor's degree by merely testing out of it.

The Benefits of CLEP and DSST Exams

First, I should answer the question: "What are CLEP and DSST Exams?" If you already know what AP exams are, they are similar. It is a test that when passed, gives the tester college credits. AP tests can only be taken by high school students. CLEPs and DSSTs are similar, except are not exclusive to high school students. Anyone can take them. Both cost $80 and there is also a fee the college charges you for using their computers; which averages about $35-$40. So each test will cost you relatively $120 to take. But let's look at this price overall. Say you have an awful pass rate of 50%, and you want to take 90 credits using the CLEP method. You also only decided to do CLEPs that award 3 credit hours each. This means 30 CLEP tests. Assuming you need to take them twice, this would translate into take 60 CLEPs/DSSTs in total. If they are $120 a piece; you would pay $7,200 in total (for 3 years of college). The fortunate thing about this is that it is also the worst-case scenario. My passing rate was about 75% and I took a total of 36 tests. Giving me 78 credit hours for $4,320. That is half the price of a semester at an in-state college for almost 3 years worth of credit.

So the biggest benefit is the wallet damage is considerably lower than the damage occurring with a normal college. Another huge benefit is the time factor. You only spend 2-3 hours a day studying for one week and you pass the test less than a week later. Then you move on to the next subject. In a normal college you take 4-7 classes at the same time for four months, cram for four exams for a week and then pass 5 months after you started. Instead take it piece by piece and in five months test out of anywhere between 15-20 classes; easily.

CLEP Tests:

So CLEP exams are considered lower-level college exams; exams to help you pass the classes you find primarily in your first two years of college. CLEPs are scored on a scale of 20 to 80 points, and most passing scores are raw 50 points. Not the same as 50%. You need about a 70% to pass. (80 X .70 = 56) But they mark it as a 50 for their odd scoring system. So if you take a practice exam and score a 50% (40 raw points) you are not ready quite yet. A huge benefit though is that whether you score a 50 or an 80 your score is the same. It is a pass/fail exam. There is no letter grade and does not count towards your GPA. Your goal with these is to get in and pass. This score varies from test to test, and college to college. For some exams, such as the world language exams, if you were to score a 60 you will get way credits (my college offered 12 credit hours).

In addition, if you do not pass the exam but you need that particular exam you can retake the exam in three months. My personal retake passing rate is 100% with CLEP and DSST exams. After you have seen the material once you get a feel for how the test will turn out the next time you attempt the exam and therefore, you will know how to study for it better.

These tests are also 100% multiple choice tests (5 options). There are NO writing portions, matching, true/false, etc. they are exclusively multiple choice tests. So the best way that you can take these exams is to go in knowing more general information instead of just word for word definitions. What this allows you to do is to make the best educated guesses possible. To add onto this, make sure you read each answer because sometimes certain answers are correct; but there can be "all of the above" options as well as answers that are more correct than others. So when you have

11

your options laid out in front of you; cross off/remove answers that are totally false, and narrow your choices down. It makes it easier to guess correctly.

Example:

What was Mussolini's first name?

A. Adolfo

B. Richard

C. Benito

D. All of the Above

So you might not remember his name but you know since he has a foreign last name, chances are his name isn't Richard and you know you can't have all of the above when not all names are available. So you remove those options either with a scratch piece of paper, or mentally…

What was Mussolini's first name?

A. Adolfo

B. ~~Richard~~

C. Benito

D. ~~All of the Above~~

Now that your answers are more narrowed down you can pick one. If you don't know go with the name that sounds best… Since I know that Hitler's name was Adolf; Mussolini's was probably not that similar so the answer must be "C" …

What was Mussolini's first name?

A. ~~Adolfo~~

B. ~~Richard~~

C. Benito

D. ~~All of the Above~~

I recommend no more than 1.5 weeks of study time for these exams. Since these are overview tests, if you spend too much time thinking about the element of pass/fail you will forget what you learned earlier on in your study period. Try not to spend more than 10 days on one CLEP test. The reason I say this is from experience; when you take too long to take your exam, you stall a little and forget important bits of information. Always study no more than 10 days and it works best. My best system was every Friday take an exam; I'd take Saturday off and study Sunday-Thursday taking the Exam on Friday. With this system my passing rate was 100%.

These tests are great for getting you out of your base courses and for allowing you to focus more time on your major courses. For me I was allowed to get more involved in my History courses and not dwell for two years on Science and Math.

DSST Tests:

DSST Tests; also called Dantes; are a little more difficult. They are considered Upper Level Courses, courses that would be taken by a junior or a senior in college, which naturally gives them a little more difficulty. These are scored on a scale of 200 to 500 with the passing score being 400. I would strongly recommend studying a little more for these. They two are pass/fail exams\. There is no letter grade and does not count towards your GPA, just like a CLEP. Your goal is the same with these: get in and pass.

13

These exams are also all multiple choice and in fact have only 4 multiple choice options to choose from; as opposed to CLEP which has 5. The questions are a little more difficult for these exams, and you will need to study a little harder for them. I recommend 1.5-2 weeks of study time. Maybe even a little more. These exams take topics more in depth, while CLEP tests the general concepts. These exams are more likely to actually count towards your major. Which is why they all tend to only award 3 credit hours.

I personally love both CLEP and DSST exams because I learned so much more studying on my own for a subject I'm interested in, instead of learning from a teacher who only can tell you what they know, in the way that is best for the entire class.

Other Options:

The only other option that I used was Straighterline.com, which allows you to do a whole course at your own pace. Basically, you still do the full college course and get a grade overall in the end. However, you can do it in any time frame you need. You can finish in a day, or in 3 years; it doesn't really matter. I actually found that I learned much less from these courses than with CLEPs and DSSTs because Straighterline isn't as much fun. There are no videos to watch, and you have to follow their format. This is because it isn't a single test, you still write papers from time to time and take chapter quizzes after assigned reading. I'm also more of a visual and auditory learner than a reading learner and their course material is all reading and no videos. I would recommend this if you are just finishing high school because you are already used to this methodology and because they have certain tests that are not offered by the CLEP and DSST program.

How I did it

So my discovery of this method came from a large array of things. My high school being one of them. One of my teachers in high school told me in one of my junior year classes about CLEP Exams. He essentially told the class that he did his Bachelor's degree in 3 years, using CLEP tests. He realized studying hard for a couple nights, taking the test and passing gave him the credits he needed. He saved time and more importantly money. So a few of my friends and I, discussed taking the exams; but, we never did.

After sometime I decided I was going to my preferred in-state school option in Colorado and I went, originally as a theater major (not a smart decision). After a few weeks of being around people complaining about the income that they will make doing theater for the rest of their lives, I began to grow tired of their pathetic cries for attention and switched my major, to international studies. And for a few more weeks I was happy. Then out of nowhere I felt the need to go back to theater but not through the same college; at the time I thought it was just a bad program. So I left my school and got a large portion of my money back. When I came home I started looking for really advanced and well known theater programs. One of which was actually in Colorado, my home state. The problem that I came across was that I couldn't start school again until the following August and it was only October. So I looked into a bunch of the schools to see if I could test out of any base courses (courses that don't focus on your major and are just the classic classes you have in school: math, science, English, etc.). So I started taking the CLEP tests to test out of my first year at one of the colleges.

After I tested out of a couple, I discovered how easy it was and I started doing more and more; passing about 60% of the time. It became addicting in a way. But this whole time, I was still focused on doing a theater school. Until one day I went online and saw an advertisement for an online school, SNHU. So I decided to research a little more into the school and discovered that the school had accepted every CLEP and DSST test you can take at the minimum acceptance scores. I got really excited, so I decided to discuss it with my parents. So the next day I asked them what I should do? Both fell silent and my dad asked me, "what do you want to do in 30 years from now." I began to respond and as I opened my mouth. He said, "No. Think about it, you don't know an answer yet." So I thought about it and eventually realized that being a theater major won't affect my outcome of theater at all and I decided on doing my school online, as a history major. I was fascinated by History and thought that it would be a good idea to have an extra skill under my belt to help me improve upon my acting. Then I took a look into the list of all the possible CLEP and DSST tests that I could take and I compiled a checklist of all the types of classes I would need to graduate. My school would allow and accept a total of up to 90 credit hours and these tests count themselves as normal hours. A sample checklist can be seen on the following page:

Course Equivalent	Exam Title	Score Needed	# of Video Lessons
PSY 108	Intro to Psych.	50	104
LIT 219	English Literature	50	114
HIS 113	U.S History I	50	108
MKT 113	Marketing	50	83
HIS 315	History of the Soviet Union	400	40+Documentaries
SOC 112	Sociology	50	116
MAT 240	Calculus	50	120

So ultimately, I only needed to take 30 credits in my school to graduate. So with my checklist of CLEP and DSST exams needed I decided to make an order. I had to do all these CLEP's and DSST's by "X" date. So I got to work, and the first few I did well on. I found a great way to study through study.com. My passing rate shot up to an 80% in the following months. There is no penalty for not passing a test so I just kept moving. The study source I used had classes incorporating video lessons. So I would watch the video lessons until it was completed and then I went to a nearby community college and took these tests at the testing center. After I finished many of my CLEP's I began doing my DSST exams (This is what I would recommend to the reader as well. Start with the easiest exams and work your way up to the harder ones). I would do the video lessons and watch documentaries on the topics. This really works for anything in the Social Science realm (especially History). Then by the end of September I had tested out of as many things as I could and was partially done with my senior year of college. Less than a year earlier I hadn't even had a single credit to my name. After that

I finished up my last seven classes and graduated less than two full years after I graduated High school.

Now I don't want to discourage people by making this seem extremely difficult because it isn't. I still was able to maintain a job, a social life, and a girlfriend simultaneously. Not exhaustingly, or with any trouble whatsoever. I would recommend this to anyone I come across because this is actually extremely easy for anybody to do. You just need to have discipline and be willing to save thousands of dollars on college.

The Best Study Materials

Now there are several great ways to study that I strongly recommend. To begin, if you are currently in high school; chances are you have classes that give you the information to test out of. For example, "Precalculus". I took a Precalculus course in my junior year of high school. I didn't start doing my CLEP exams until over two years later so I had to relearn all of my study material for the Precalculus exam. Grant it, I learned the material much faster and was able to be prepared at a much quicker pace; due to the fact that it was all review. So if you are currently in a course that is similar, take a practice exam and see if you are ready. Then pass without really even having to study. This especially applies to AP exams; because AP exams have many course equivalencies with CLEP; remember the CLEP tests are shorter and easier to pass. So take these instead of your AP exam and pass at a higher rate and at any time of the year. Plus you find out if you pass directly after you take it.

CLEP Official Study Guide:

This is something I recommend to anybody who needs practice exams to test their skills in a subject. You can get this on Amazon, but your best bet is the CLEP website. The book is $25 in total which is not a lot considering it gives you every practice exam with answers following the exam.

Now the only downside to this study guide is, for your language tests as it doesn't supply the audio recordings. However, it does allow you to read your audio recordings to see if you at least know the words and phrases.

Study.com:

This is my preferred site. You will see me recommend it in my section on 'How I did it, 'constantly. It is the best when it comes to being able to learn the materials for the CLEP and DSST testing instantly. Quick side note though is that it does NOT help with the French or German exams; only Spanish.

This site has college professors making video lessons on a sizeable array of topics in videos that are anywhere from 4-12 minutes a piece. Each video is followed by a brief quiz allowing the student to grasp how well you have learned the video you just watched. If you don't do well, just go and re-watch the video.

Now the reason that I believe this site is so good is that it is taught by college professors through video lessons. Each professor is trained in their field and knows how to properly study for the subject you are trying to learn. The video aspect allows you to gain a visual to understand the material on a deeper level, as opposed to just reading the material.

Also the site divides their lessons into folders that are actually titled by CLEP and DSST titles. For example, if you are looking to study the" Introduction to Psychology" exam you just simply search it and the whole course will come up; divided into chapters that have 4-20 lessons each. Every chapter has a test at the end to test the knowledge of your material. This program is what gave me such a high passing rate because I was able to organize my thoughts better and have somebody explain to me the true simplicity of each subject.

This is the study program I used the most and in fact on 12 of the exams I passed, it was the only site I used the whole time and with it you can virtually take anywhere from 1-5 tests in one month (I averaged about 3-4 per month). The only downside to this program is that it is $100 per month. Even though it was more expensive my passing rate with this site actually almost doubled and that saved me two failed exams per month (which is $240 saved from this site). I would strongly recommend this site to anybody wanting to pass quickly and more efficiently.

Instacert:

Now I have not personally used Instacert but I have heard good things about it. From what I have gathered about this site, it is just flashcards that are focused on helping you study for your CLEP and DSST Exams. It's $20 per month and because of that I wouldn't use it. You can get free online flash cards with Quizlet. Which is the other site that can be used for flash cards, and my preference of the two.

Quizlet:

Now the reason why my preference in flash cards is through Quizlet is because it is free. It is another flash card site but the beauty is that millions of college students from the past decade have been using it. So you can find any topic you are looking to study and study those flashcards. You can also make your own on either the application or the website; instead of having to buy cards from a store. You can also organize countless different sets of words into your own folders so that you don't lose track of your topics. It is still absolutely free and can be assessed on a computer or as an app on your phone.

Library:

I am honestly surprised that people do not take advantage of the library more often than they currently do. You can get documentaries, books, audio books, and movies there. It is typically one of the best places to go to gain any amount of knowledge you want. It is also FREE. If you're a busy person and don't really have time for studying, get audiobooks on library CDs and pop them in while driving; you'll learn so quality material in a short amount of time. I would definitely recommend the library; even if you only use it as a secondary studying source. Still use it.

Duolingo:

I am in love with Duolingo for learning languages because it makes it fun. It is absolutely free and the language CLEPs are valuable. Most colleges offer anywhere between 9-16 credits on the language exams which do not cost any more money than a normal test.

The way Duolingo is set up is as a tree that allows you to study new words once you have completed easier lessons. They also keep track of your daily streak while you are on the site. CLEP offers tests in Spanish, French, and German; which are all languages on the Duolingo site. You can compete with your friends.

To add, I strongly believe that if you know your full Duolingo tree for any of the three languages, you will pass the CLEP exam. This site can be used by anybody who wants to brush up on their language skills or totally start from square one.

I personally started from square one and have now become fluent in German through the site and a few other things as well. You can use the website or the app on your phone. Each language tree on the site is built by native speakers of the language you want to learn so you truly know what you are learning.

The only difficulty with learning languages for CLEPs is that they take time, because naturally languages have a lot of material to cover. So what I did is I took my German CLEP after I took every other CLEP exam and studied through Duolingo the whole time. This way I could fully complete my tree and then pass the examination less than nine months later.

Mango Languages:

I also really enjoyed Mango, which is a free app run through the Library in the United States. That also will help you with any of the three languages you need to know for the CLEP exam. While Duolingo helps you learn vocabulary, Mango helps with grammar and listening. You will learn your words and grammar in a context in which will give you the cultural notes helping you to remember when to properly use certain words. Also it is a really fun site that is very helpful for learning languages.

YouTube:

YouTube has countless sources of knowledge. Many professors leave their lectures up from their classes all over YouTube. You can watch their full lectures from the actual class; over and over if need be. There are also many YouTubers who release their own lessons, which can supplement what you have learned from the professors. You can also find a large array of documentaries that can be incredibly helpful in your studies. YouTube is also a free site and is nice because, well, you don't have to pay anything. One downside though is that you do not really always know how accurate the information is. Anybody can post anything they want. I recommend steering clear of any sites that do not have many people following it.

Phone Apps:

Now many apps can be downloaded that will help you study for your exam. This is actually what I did before study.com. You can download free apps that can help you know more about your topic. Not the best option but this still can be helpful from time to time; especially on easier CLEP exams.

School Acceptance of Exams

With this section I have compiled a list of school acceptance of CLEP/ DSST exams. Something that tends to be a common theme through this is, online schools or schools that are not big schools with a lot of students or big sports teams accept exams more often. The smaller the school the more they tend to accept exams. However, this is not always the case. I personally did my degree through Southern New Hampshire University, which is a great school when it comes to accepting exams. They allow up to 90 transferred credits and accept every exam at the ACE recommended score; which is the lowest possible score that any college can accept.

Following is a list of colleges that accept every CLEP and DSST exam you can take. So if you want to only do CLEPs/DSSTs you could try:

- Excelsior College
- Thomas Edison State College
- Charter Oak State College

For any college you would be interested in looking at you will have to go to the college's website and find out exactly what their rule is over the exams. The four I recommended are great options and I would recommend all of them.

How to Take an Exam?

Now something that you need to understand in taking these exams above all else is; the power of positive thinking. What I mean by this is, the most important factor to passing these exams is to not doubt yourself and constantly reassure yourself that you have prepared enough, and will therefore; undoubtedly pass your exam. The reason that I say this is because of my own personal experience with the exams; both DSSTs and CLEPs. Every time that I was nervous about passing; or better yet, worried about failing I failed. EVERY. SINGLE. TIME. But every time I was prepared (translation: I had put in the requisite study time) and ready and confident to pass the exam I would pass.

How to Order a CLEP Exam:

So to be able to take an exam you must do a couple things. Find a community college or a college nearby that you can use as a testing center. A couple things to be aware of with this: check the sitting fee for a college before jumping into their school and paying excessive amounts of money, and find the cheapest option. Also check to see if they offer the exam you are looking to take because certain exams are not possible at certain colleges.

1. Go to the clep.collegeboard website. This is completely vital because this is the only way to purchase the exam. Which you can NOT purchase at the testing center.

2. Purchase the exam you desire from the college board website and PRINT OUT your ticket. If you don't print out your ticket you won't be able to check in for your exam and will have wasted $80 on nothing. Buy the exam and make sure

you pick your college you want your scores sent to when you purchase. This way you don't have to pay extra to have your scores sent to a college campus. If you do not know where you are going yet you can always pay the $25 fee to send your CLEP transcript to the college of your choosing on a later date.

3. Sign up at the college site that you choose to schedule your exam time. Most colleges require that you schedule 24 hours in advance to insure that they can fit you in. Also rescheduling is not an issue. Reschedule whenever you need to. It will not cost you anything; in fact, I've yet to see a college charge to have me reschedule one of my exams.

4. Go and take the Exam; you can not bring anything into the exam. The testing center is required to supply scratch paper and a pencil. If you do a math exam you do not need to bring anything, the calculator is programmed into the computer and the testing center will confiscate your calculator anyway.

5. Pass. Anyone can and I believe that anybody has the ability to pass with ease.

Also try to keep your exam testing center consistent. The reason why is because the people who work there get to know you the more you come and will try to get you in faster so you can take your test quicker. This actually happened to me, there was a long line and one of the women who knew me let me cut the whole thing and get in with in the next five minutes.

How to Order a DSST Exam:

This one is a tad different than CLEP exams for ordering. The first step is virtually the same with one emphasized element: most colleges do not offer the DSST for Public Speaking. It is much rarer to find in this case, but most exams are offered at community colleges.

1. Find the testing center that offers your exam. If you already have a location that you take your CLEPs at, if they take DSST exams too I recommend taking your DSST exams there as well. Again the reason is so that you can build a friendship with the testing administrators and thus gain quicker access to the exam room.

2. Study for the Exam you desire.

3. Bring a credit/debit card to your exam on exam day. The reason why is because you purchase your ticket from the computer.

4. When you get to the testing center create an account. I forgot my username and password almost every single time I took a DSST exam so I always just created a new account.

5. Buy your exam on your newly created account.

6. Pass your exam.

Now again I want to emphasize that the best way to pass these exams is positivity. Always believe you will pass your exam, and then you will.

A Good Studying Routine:

My favorite site to use is definitely study.com. The way it operates is by giving you short videos to watch and then gives you 5 question quizzes at the end so that you can judge your knowledge gained from the exam. It is a nice because it actually compiles the videos needed to be studied in order to pass your CLEP and DSST exams, and are labeled in their own folders. Some recommendations from me when you use this site:

1. Watch each video beginning to end. Even if you feel like you know one of the lessons or if you already watched it for another exam. Always re-watch it. I found that when I watched all of the videos from beginning to end, I passed with a much higher rate.

2. Try to watch all of the videos in your exam folder in no more than two weeks. The reason that I say this is because, you will start to forget things the longer you put off taking the exam.

Now to be clear, this is not for everybody. It does cost about $100 per month and if you are not willing to pay that amount my best recommendation is your local library. Find the exam you want to take and find all the parts of the subject you need to know on those topics. Then grab books off of the bookshelves or find documentaries that can help you with those studies.

After you're done studying the most important thing to do is relax. Do not stress about it. You can always take the exam again. Also you will fail on occasion and you have to be willing and understand that failure is a normal process of life. It isn't about failing; I failed 25% of my tests; however, my passing rate on exams I took a second time is 100%. Get up and do it again. The one thing about taking an exam again is that you have to wait 3 months to be able to (for both CLEP and DSST).

Next with the checklist that you have created go over to the box of the test you are taking before you leave; and point at the title and say, "I will check this off today." Reassurance is a huge key to help you pass this exam.

Also try to avoid taking the test first thing in the morning, the best time is midday so you feel well rested and prepared to the best of your abilities.
WARNING!!!!!!: DON'T CRAM THE DAY OF YOUR EXAM, Don't even study right before, you will over stress and be more forgetful when you are over worried. Relax and pass. You can study with the simple schedule that I have outlined below.

Monday: Study 1-2 hours

Tuesday: Study 2-3 hours

Wednesday: Study 3-4 hours

Thursday: Take Practice exam; base study habits for this day on score

Friday: Take Test (do not study, if you are studying you aren't ready)

Now for the last portion; take your exam early on from when you wake up. Now to be clear, if you are used to waking up at 10am don't force yourself to wake up at an earlier time like 8 am, but instead schedule your test for 11 am. The reason for this is because just after you wake up is when your brain will be the freshest. You'll have your breakfast or coffee, or whatever you need, and your brain will not be exhausted from the day.

My Personal View on Exams I Took
CLEP Exams:

Now before you read all of my personal reviews on exams I feel as if you should know that I did not take every CLEP and DSST exam possible, I only took the ones that I have listed below. There are a multitude of other tests that you can take on these topics, which you can find on the exam websites. But below I have described each test's format, how I studied for these exams, my difficulty rating on a scale of 1 to 10 (1 being easiest, 10 being hardest), and my personal view on the test itself. Recall, your classes and therefore the tests you take to complete these classes depend on your degree requirements.

Now the way that I studied for the large portion of my exams was through study.com. I recommend this site again because of the way it operates. It has teachers teach short video lessons that are on average 8-10 minutes, after each of them you take a short 5-8 question quiz to see if you grasped the material. These video lessons are divided into chapters, which all have a short test towards the end of them. After you complete all of the chapters you take a practice exam, which tells you if you are likely to pass or fail your actual exam. The one downside to this is that it costs $100 per month to use. But I assure you it is well worth it. So if I leave a section blank or shortly written upon, chances are I studied for that exam with study.com.

History of the United States I:
Overview of the Test/Test Format:
Topical Specifications
35% Political institutions, political developments, behavior, and public policy
25% Social issues and progress
10% Economic progress
15% Cultural and intellectual developments
15% Diplomacy and international relations

Chronological Specifications
30% 1500–1789
70% 1790–1877

How I Studied for this Exam:
I used study.com for this exam. I am also extremely addicted to the history channel and their documentaries; that was a great help for me in studying for this exam. I would recommend both of these sites for any exam you desire (mainly history with the history channel).

The Mason Difficulty Rating:
3 out of 10 (fairly easy)

My Personal Review on the Test:
This exam is very easy to take. I studied less than 4 days for this exam and passed on my first attempt. Most high schools teach this material in a sophomore or junior level history class. If you have forgotten all about this topic, it is a vague history of the early United States. It is often a required basic   course for many history majors, counting towards one of the major credits. If not a history major, you are often required to take this as a base course that could fall under the social sciences. I love history so I am naturally more inclined to studying it. But it was not difficult to learn from.

History of the United States II:
Overview of the Test/Test Format:
Topical Specifications
5%:Political institutions, behavior, and public policy

5%:Social developments

0%:Economic developments

5%:Cultural and intellectual developments

5%:Diplomacy and international relations

Chronological Specifications
0%:1865–1914

0%:1915–present

How I Studied for this Exam:
Again for this exam I used study.com and the history channel. Which again I

would both strongly recommend.

The Mason Difficulty Rating:
4 out of 10 (Relatively Easy)

My Personal Review on the Test:
Now this exam is almost exactly like the first one in difficulty, except it is the

other half of the United States' History. It is also not extremely difficult either. Do not

underestimate this exam entirely though. I considered myself really knowledgeable on

his topic the first time I took it; consequently, I did not study at all and I did not pass.

However, when I took it the second time I actually studied and passed with little to no

difficulty. Note; the trick is again not luck but actual study time.

Introduction to Psychology:
Overview of the Test/Test Format:

8–9%: History, Approaches, Methods
8–9%: Biological Bases of Behavior
7–8%: Sensation and Perception
5–6%: States of Consciousness
10–11%: Learning
8–9%: Cognition
7–8%: Motivation and Emotion
8–9%: Developmental Psychology
7–8%: Personality
8–9%: Psychological disorders and health
7–8%: Treatment of psychological disorders
7–8%: Social Psychology
3–4%: Statistics, Tests, and Measurement

Now as you can see there is a plethora lot of topics that are needed to be covered to pass this exam. It means that the test is actually fairly easy as it is just a primer. The reason for this is that the topics are introductory and not deep. So instead of knowing which part of the brain is operating during a bipolar person's malfunction all you need to know is the names of psychologists and their basic contributions to the field of psychology.

How I Studied for this Exam:

I also studied for this exam through study.com solely. This is a topic I was completely unfamiliar with and received the proper education on the topic from study.com.

The Mason Difficulty Rating:
2 out of 10 (Easy)

My Personal Review on the Test:

One of the most common misconceptions about this exam is that it is too difficult because there is so much to cover in one test. The topics are just introductory knowledge; essentially one is learning the definitions and not much more. Knowing the psychologists alone, will probably get you a passing grade. It was not difficult and I had an easy time studying for it.

Introduction to Sociology:

Overview of the Test/Test Format:

20%: Institutions
10%: Social Patterns
25%: Social Processes
25%: Social Stratification (Process and Structure)
20%: The Sociological Perspective

How I Studied for this Exam:

This exam is very similar to the Psychology exam, lots of vague topics. I again used study.com for this exam, and I just watched all the way through. I needed no other amount of studying for this test.

The Mason Difficulty Rating:

3 out of 10 (fairly easy)

My Personal Review on the Test:

Now this exam was by no means difficult. I almost passed without studying because it is not a super complicated subject. All the material is more of an overview of the subject than an actual in depth analysis on social topics. It's also actually a really interesting course and I would recommend it because the people in it are actually really entertaining to study (largely because they are just so, incredibly insane).

Western Civilization I:

Overview of the Test/Test Format:
%–10%: Ancient Near East
5%–17%: Ancient Greece and Hellenistic Civilization
5%–17%: Ancient Rome
3%–27%: Medieval History
3%–17%: Renaissance and Reformation
0%–15%: Early Modern Europe, 1560-1648

How I Studied for this Exam:
Similar to the other two history exams. I used my knowledge of history from the history channel, as well as, study.com and I passed easily.

The Mason Difficulty Rating:
3 out of 10 (fairly easy)

My Personal Review on the Test:
This exam might be more difficult for me to give my opinion on because I am biased towards history. However, this was a pretty easy exam. It covers a lot of topics but not the specifics of those topics. Definitely would recommend because of the vagueness of the topic. This comment actually applies towards any CLEP/DSST one wants to take. If you want easier exams, take exams on topics that are much vaguer. They are much easier and well worth the free credits.

Western Civilization II:

Overview of the Test/Test Format:
7%–9%: Absolutism and Constitutionalism, 1648–1715
4%–6%: Competition for empire and economic expansion
5%–7%: The scientific view of the world
7%–9%: Period of Enlightenment
10%–13%: Revolution and Napoleonic Europe
7%–9%: The Industrial Revolution
6%–8%: Political and cultural developments, 1815–1848
8%–10%: Politics and diplomacy in the Age of Nationalism, 1850–1914
7%–9%: Economy, culture, and imperialism, 1850–1914
10%–12%: The First World War and the Russian Revolution
7%–9%: Europe between the wars
8%-10%: The Second World War and contemporary Europe

How I Studied for this Exam:
Again similar to the other history exams I had taken. I used my knowledge of history from the history channel documentaries, as well as, study.com and I passed easily.

The Mason Difficulty Rating:
3 out of 10 (fairly easy)

My Personal Review on the Test:
A theme that I noticed while taking these exams, note the titles of these classes. Essentially, one takes the first semester Western Civ and then the second semester. In other words, if you pass Western Civilization 1 you could use the same attitude of studying you used and then pass Western Civilization 2. Again the test is relatively easy, and I would recommend it for anybody who needs it, or anyone who enjoys history.

American Government:

Overview of the Test/Test Format:
30%–35%: Institutions and Policy Processes: Presidency, Bureaucracy, and Congress
5%–20%: Federal Courts, Civil Liberties, and Civil Rights
5%–20%: Political Parties and Interest Groups
10%–15%: Political Beliefs and Behavior
5%–20%: Constitutional Underpinnings of American Democracy

How I Studied for this Exam:
Now I studied for this exam in a number of ways. I of course used study.com, like I did for most of my tests. But I also took AP government in high school and did not pass the exam. So I took the CLEP instead. Because I did not study, I failed it again. I also rushed it because I was looking for elective credits and not as an actual course.

The Mason Difficulty Rating:
5 out of 10 (average difficulty)

My Personal Review on the Test:
So my problem with this exam came down to a few factors. The main one being I rushed it. Something I cannot emphasize enough with CLEP and DSST exams. DO NOT RUSH. Almost every single time I rushed I failed (translation; did not study) and by a decent margin too. If I studied this there is no way, I would have failed. The only reason this score is as high as it is, is because I didn't pass; therefore I don't feel I have the right to say it was easy.

Macroeconomics:

Overview of the Test/Test Format:
8–12%: Basic Economic Concepts
12–16%: Measurement of Economic Performance
15–20%: National Income and Price Determination
15–20%: Financial Sector
20–25%: Inflation, Unemployment, and Stabilization Policies
5–10%: Economic Growth and Productivity
9-13%: Open Economy: International Trade and Finance

How I Studied for this Exam:
Again this exam was studied for through study.com, and similar to the

American Government exam, I had this course in high school. However, again this is

not one of the exams I passed because I rushed. I did not follow my own rules. Or

what are they teaching in high school?

The Mason Difficulty Rating:
6 out of 10 (moderately difficult)

My Personal Review on the Test:
So this exam is an interesting one to say the least. It is a more difficult exam

because for me it was a totally new subject. With a math exam your previous math

knowledge is always helpful, but with Macro you are learning information you have

likely never touched before. This is not one of my passing tests, I actually had a period

of failure for about 4 exams straight, because I was rushing so much. I was attempting

to finish earlier than I actually could have; therefore, I did not pass.

Calculus:

Overview of the Test/Test Format:
0%: Limits
40%: Integral Calculus
0%: Differential Calculus

How I Studied for this Exam:
Again I used study.com for this exam but I would not recommend this subject

to anyone that either does not need it, or has never taken a calculus course. This exam

felt like learning a foreign language, and was extremely difficult to pass.

The Mason Difficulty Rating:
8 out of 10 (difficult)

My Personal Review on the Test:
Do NOT take this exam unless it is required or you have taken this class in the

past. This exam is extremely difficult and I would not recommend it if you do not fall

into one of the two categories listed above. After taking this exam, I felt as if I truly

knew nothing on the topic and this is the only exam that I took that I believe you can

not learn on your own; that you would actually need a teacher to learn this information.

Precalculus:

Overview of the Test/Test Format:
20%: Algebraic Expressions, Equations, and Inequalities
15%: Functions: Concept, Properties, and Operations
30%: Representations of Functions: Symbolic, Graphical, and Tabular
10%: Analytic Geometry
15%: Trigonometry and its Applications
10%: Functions as Models

How I Studied for this Exam:
The knowledge I gained for this exam came from the fact that I took this course my junior year of high school. If you can take this before you graduate high school. If not, you can just review the material. You can find it almost anywhere online and again study.com will be very helpful in this field.

The Mason Difficulty Rating:
1 out of 10 (walk in the park)

My Personal Review on the Test:
This is one of those tests that is something you can do if you were take the high school equivalency course on this subject. That is exactly what I did for this exam I took this course my junior year of high school and ended up taking this exam two years afterwards. I needed a quick refresher of the information, but directly afterwards was ready for the test. Ready with only a couple weeks of studying. This is a great way to get a math credit in college which many people need for their base courses. Definitely would recommend this exam because it is high school junior and senior level material. In fact, if you are taking the class in high school currently, once you finish your final go directly to take this test. You should pass with flying colors.

College Composition Modular:
Overview of the Test/Test Format:
0%: Conventions of Standard Written English
0%: Revision Skills, Including Sentence-Level Skills
5%: Ability to Use Source Materials
5%: Rhetorical Analysis

How I Studied for this Exam:
This was one of the few exams that I took prior to my discovery of study.com; and it required no great effort. It was one of the first CLEPs I took and I took it only a few months after graduating high school. Most high schools teach the level of English you will need to know for this test and I would strongly recommend it because it does get you out of your English credits.

The Mason Difficulty Rating:
2 out of 10 (easy)

My Personal Review on the Test:
I would definitely recommend taking this exam. Some degree programs require an English credit class. It is easy and well worth an attempt.

English Literature:
Overview of the Test/Test Format:

35%-40%: Knowledge of:

- Literary background
- Identification of authors
- Metrical patterns
- Literary references
- Literary terms

60%-65%: Ability to:

- Analyze the elements of form in a literary passage
- Perceive meanings
- Identify tone and mood
- Follow patterns of imagery
- Identify characteristics of style
- Comprehend the reasoning in an excerpt of literary criticism

How I Studied for this Exam:

This exam I used study.com for and it is a relatively easy test. It is an interesting subject and the information isn't brand new. You might have either already read the poems and books at school or in your own life. Study.com is again a great source to use.

The Mason Difficulty Rating:
3 out of 10 (fairly easy)

My Personal Review on the Test:

So with any exam that is a 100 level course (freshman level) you will mostly hear the same thing from me over and over again: take it. These exams almost always count as base courses and you will pass them a lot. They're simple exams that anybody can take and pass with just some study time.

American Literature:

Overview of the Test/Test Format:
5%: The Colonial and Early National Period (Beginnings-1830)
5%: The Romantic Period (1830-1870)
0%: The Period of Realism and Naturalism (1870-1910)
5%: The Modernist Period (1910-1945)
5%: The Contemporary Period (1945-Present)

How I Studied for this Exam:
Again for this exam I used study.com. This exam has different information

from English Literature exam as if focuses on American Literature. So instead of

studying Keats, one studies Whitman. But it is just as easy with a very similar format.

The Mason Difficulty Rating:
3 out of 10 (fairly easy)

My Personal Review on the Test:
Again with exams that have multiple versions of the same exam (English

Literature and American Literature) all you have to do is study the same way you did

for one as you do for the other. These tests are made by the same company and are

tested in an extremely similar way.

Humanities:

Overview of the Test/Test Format:
50%: Literature
50%: The Arts

How I Studied for this Exam:

This is one of the exams I actually did not use study.com for. I used an app I found on my phone, and began just playing the games on it. This was actually prior to finding study.com and I still passed well above the passing grade.

The Mason Difficulty Rating:
2 out of 10 (easy)

My Personal Review on the Test:
With this exam I had very little trouble with it but also I did theater throughout high school so I was at an advantage going into the exam. However, most of this is just quick memorizing, and not difficult concepts. You'll need to know specific titles of art and composers; however it is not difficult at all.

College Mathematics and College Algebra:
Overview of the Test/Test Format:
0%: Algebra and Functions
0%: Counting and Probability
5%: Data Analysis and Statistics
0%: Financial Mathematics
0%: Geometry
5%: Logic and Sets
0%: Numbers

How I Studied for this Exam:
The reason that I combined these two exams is because they are basically the exact same exam. If you know you can pass one of them, take both on the same day, because they are the same test. I actually did not study for either of these exams because I learned the difficult material in my Precalculus class in High school. However, there are many sites all over the internet that you could use. I took Pre calc, Algebra 1 and 11 in High School. If you do not have this background, you will need to take an easier math class first.

The Mason Difficulty Rating:
1 out of 10 (walk in the park)

My Personal Review on the Test:
The thing that I have always absolutely loved about math multiple choice tests, is that if you don't get one of the suggested answers you know it is wrong. These exams are too easy to pass up, and if your school offers both of them, take both and get out of math class as soon as you can.

Principles of Marketing:
Overview of the Test/Test Format:
8%–13%: Role of Marketing in Society
17%–24%: Role of Marketing in a Firm
22%–27%: Target Marketing
40%–50%: Marketing Mix

How I Studied for this Exam:
Now this exam I studied for in a couple of ways. A big one is I took up a summer job with CUTCO knives; it paid decent money, and they gave us a required marketing class at the beginning. This was extremely helpful for me, and it was also a free education. CUTCO is always looking for employees and will always allow you to learn from them. I again also used study.com for this test as well, to make sure that my knowledge was at it's fullest potential for this test.

The Mason Difficulty Rating:
2 out of 10 (easy)

My Personal Review on the Test:
So with this test I knew a lot of the information preceding the test. That also being said my opinion might be a tad skewed towards my beliefs. It is by no means difficult because it is an easy test to break down. Many of the answer options fit common sense ideas when you read them. So you can narrow the information down relatively quick. Still study if you need to for this exam; however, don't be too worried

Social Sciences and History:

Overview of the Test/Test Format:

0%: History
        13-15%: Western Civilization
        13-15%: World History
0%: Economics
0%: Geography
0%: Government/Political Science

How I Studied for this Exam:

This is a tricky answer because the truth is I didn't. Here is what I mean. I took all the other history CLEPs, and the social science CLEPs first. This is all knowledge that you'll need to know for this exam. The only difference is that it makes use of prior classes and then adds to them. For this test, I looked at the practice exam and and knew most of the answers, and decided just to take the exam the next day, and passed with flying colors.

The Mason Difficulty Rating:

1 out of 10 (walk in the park)

My Personal Review on the Test:

If you need elective credits and have already taken Intro to Psych, Intro to Sociology, and the four history CLEPs, you don't need to study for this exam. All that you need is to go in and take it. You will pass. It isn't difficult at all. It is such a generalized test that you could have common knowledge and probably still pass. The reason that I say this is because anytime I pass a test with a 60 or higher, it means that it isn't very difficult. This was one of the few that I passed with such a high score.

German Language (Information also applies for French and Spanish):

Overview of the Test/Test Format:

40%: Sections I and II: Listening; conversations and spoken paragraphs with relatively easy grammar and Vocabulary. Spoken at about A2-B1 Fluency

60%: Section III: Reading; Harder vocabulary and grammar, however, you can read it multiple times and take your time reading the words as opposed to only hearing them.

How I Studied for this Exam:

Alright this part will be longer since I used so many materials to study for this exam. I used six different study sources for this exam which I have separated into the paragraphs below.

Duolingo Use if you want to learn a language from scratch and for free. It is a free app/website that you can use just by logging in with your Facebook. Duolingo is based on the concept of building upon your natural language. Instead of just reading a book in German and googling word by word and figuring them out, it takes you through a tree and teaches you interesting topics along the way. Building on new types of vocabulary, such as business or sports; I used this tree and kept reviewing the information for about nine months before I passed the exam.

Another great site is **Mango**. Mango is also a free app for your phone that you can download. The libraries in the U.S developed it and I found that this was a big help with my grammar skills. It concentrates on basic vocabulary that is extremely helpful for your exam and it also has a creative extras part. So for German I learned vocabulary that I would use in Oktoberfest.

FluentU is another great site to use. The only down side is that it does cost $15 a month. It operates is by showing you videos with subtitles, and whenever you have any confusion you can just hover your mouse over the subtitle and know what the word means. This is very helpful especially with listening comprehension, it broadened my vocabulary and allowed me to fully grasp the information better. It also helps with one's accent.

Mixxer is another great site to use. Mixxer allows you to connect with people in foreign countries that are seeking to learn English, so you help them with English and in return they'll help you with German, French, Spanish, etc. I do really like this site. It helps to be able to speak the language with native speakers. Once you have learned basic vocabulary listening and trying to construct a sentence with a native speaker is infectious.

German phone apps are a great source for expanding your German vocabulary, especially with every day expressions and terms. It's very helpful to be able to read and identify words you don't necessarily hear from a conversation. For example, how often do you use the word "cloud" every day. But at least you know what it means to benefit you in the future. For the test this is very useful.

YouTube is absolutely the best source for learning grammar. Grammar is probably one of the most difficult parts about German, but luckily there are many people all over the internet who help people learn German Grammar and words. This also helps a lot with listening comprehension skills. One of my favorite YouTubers for German, is Learn German with Anja. She has a slightly dorky personality, but was easily the biggest help I had on my grammar knowledge.

Songs/books are probably one of the best things to use. You become so open to new vocabulary, and foreign singers. My recommendation is to find a band you really like in that language (which really is not difficult) and listen to them frequently.

Also, we have Dr. Seuss, and they have their own unique versions of children's books which are really fun to read, and will teach you a lot of new words, my personal favorite is <u>Der Struwwelpeter</u> by: Heinrich Hoffman. It is a much older book; but, is so morbid and dark it doesn't seem like a children's book.

The Mason Difficulty Rating:
9 out of 10 (really difficult)

My Personal Review on the Test:

Now I implore you to not be disheartened from my high rating; the reason I gave it a higher rating is because it is not easy to learn a language in a week, like many of the other tests. So you must take your time with this. The first time I took the test was seven months after I beginning German, and I didn't pass by one point. However, you will never fail the second time so I retook it 3 months later and ended passing the test by a lot. This was in part do to my irritation from barely not passing the first time. I recommend this exam or either of the other language exams to anybody. If you speak one of these languages already, just go take it. It is not expensive and it could even give you a feel as to how your German (French or Spanish) is coming along. If you don't know any language, like myself at the time, you will easily learn it if you take your time and don't over stress about the exam results. It offers a lot of credits so it will be a harder exam.

DSST Exams:

The Civil War and Reconstruction:

Overview of the Test/Test Format:
6%: Causes of the War
1%: The war fought in 1861
7%: The war fought in 1862
9%: The war fought in 1863
5%: The war fought in 1864
%: The war fought in 1865
5%: The Reconstruction Period

How I Studied for this Exam:
Now this exam is not fully covered by study.com; so in addition to using this website I also watched many documentaries from all over the internet, as well as ocumentaries from the library. The Library is a great source for any type of knowledge ou want. Including audio books that you can listen to while you're driving in the car to elp you understand better. I would strongly recommend using the library.

The Mason Difficulty Rating:
6 out of 10 (moderately difficult)

My Personal Review on the Test:
This exam is definitely an interesting one. I thought myself to be somewhat nowledgeable on the Civil War prior to this exam but I found it to be so much more dvanced than I expected. It is not an easy test and in fact the first time I took it I did ot pass. With DSST exams as a whole, they are more difficult to pass; therefore, equire more study time. This exam is definitely worth it to take if it could apply owards your degree, but otherwise you will be taking an extra class with a lot of course oad.

Substance Abuse:

Overview of the Test/Test Format:
12%: Overview of Substance Abuse and Dependence
6%: Classification of Drugs
9%: Pharmacological and Neurophysiological Principles
14%: Alcohol
6%: Anti-Anxiety, Sedative and Hypnotics
5%: Inhalants
10%: Tobacco and Nicotine
6%: Psychomotor
7%: Opioids
10%: Cannabinoids
4%: Hallucinogens
4%: Other Drugs of Abuse
3%: Antipsychotic Drugs
4%: Antidepressants and Mood Stabilizers

How I Studied for this Exam:
Probably you can see the pattern that with so many of these exams I used

study.com I would still recommend it until the day I die. As a source for learning it is

great all around. With this subject anybody can study with library books as well. There

is a lot of information on drug topics as it is a pressing issue.

The Mason Difficulty Rating:
4 out of 10 (relatively easy)
My Personal Review on the Test:
So the thing that makes this exam so good is that it is an interesting topic.

When studying this I gained so much knowledge about so many different drugs and

problems caused from drugs, that I never knew existed. This is one of those tests that I

would just recommend taking, because it is relatively easy and most people don't have

trouble with the subject. Also any subject that is at all interesting, you will pass

excessively more often.

Criminal Justice & Introduction to Law Enforcement:

These two exams are almost the same, the study material is slightly different,

but I guarantee, whatever score you get on one exam, you will get close to the same

score on the other exam. The test format below is for the Law Enforcement exam, just

so you aren't confused.

Overview of the Test/Test Format:

%: History of Law Enforcement

2%: Overview of United States Criminal Justice System and Process

5%: Law Enforcement Systems in the United States

0%: Law Enforcement Organization, Management and Issues

5% Criminal and Constitutional Law and Precedents

How I Studied for this Exam:

Again for these exams I used study.com as well as a lot of library

documentaries. These tests, should be studied for and taken together because it'll be

easier and you'll get more credits.

The Mason Difficulty Rating:

6 out of 10 (moderately difficult)

My Personal Review on the Test:

These tests are relatively easy. If you study all the information being asked for,

you should have absolutely no problem on this exam. Studying for DSSTs seems to be

more interesting for me, and I hope it is for you as well. In comparison to CLEPs you

have more details which make the topic interesting. So if you are looking for an

fascinating topic, I would strongly recommend these two exams because it will give the

average American an appreciation for how our legal system works.

World Religions:

Overview of the Test/Test Format:
5%: Definition and Origins of Religion
5%: Indigenous Religions
11%: Hinduism
11%: Buddhism
6%: Confucianism
4%: Taoism
4%: Shintoism
11%: Judaism
18% Christianity
16%: Islam
9%: Religious Movements and Syncretism

How I Studied for this Exam:
This exam is also not fully covered by study.com; so in addition to using this website I also watched a few documentaries from all over the Internet; my study regimen for this was similar to the other DSST exams I had taken. The Library is a great source for any type of knowledge you want. Including audio books that you can listen to while you're driving in the car and help you understand better. I know I sound like a broken record but the library during this time is your best friend.

The Mason Difficulty Rating:
2 out of 10 (easy)

My Personal Review on the Test:
So this exam was really easy for me because I went to a Christian high school, in which, I studied most of these religions on my own, so I could increase my arguments. In other words, I might have some bias in this topic. However, the exam itself is not difficult. You should definitely know the beliefs of all of these religions. However, they won't ask you to quote scriptures or anything along those lines. Just know the general beliefs and historical overviews of these religions and you'll pass with flying colors.

History of the Vietnam War:

Overview of the Test/Test Format:

%: Vietnam before 1940

% World War II, the Cold War, and the First Indochina War (1940-1955)

0%: Diem and Nation-State Building

0%: LBJ Americanizes the War

0%: America takes Charge

%: Home Front USA

%: Tet Offensive

0% Vietnamizing the War

%: The War at Home

%: Cambodia and Laos

% A Decent Interval of Ceasefire

%: U.S. Legacies and Lessons

How I Studied for this Exam:

The way that I studied for this exam is the way I studied for the large portion of my exams; through study.com. And again I would recommend this site because of the way that it operates. It has teachers teach short video lessons that are on average 8-10 minutes, after each of them you take a short 5-8 question quiz to see if you grasped the material. These video lessons are divided into chapters, which all have a short test towards the end of them. After you complete all of the chapters you take a practice exam, which tells you if you are likely to pass or fail your actual exam. The one downside to this is that it costs $100 per month to use. But I assure you is well worth it.

Now this exam is not fully covered by study.com; so in addition to using this website I also watched many documentaries from all over the internet, as well as documentaries from the library. The Library is a great source for any type of knowledge you want. Including audio books that you can listen to while you're driving in the car and help you understand better. I would strongly recommend using the library.

The Mason Difficulty Rating:
3 out of 10 (fairly easy)

My Personal Review on the Test:

Out of all of the exams I took, this was one of my all time favorites because while I was growing up I was always hearing about how bad the war was, but being able to learn the actual details was fascinating to me. The details that are on this war make it all the more interesting, and the fact that most people only a generation older than mine were alive during that time period. It is a fascinating topic.

History of the Soviet Union:

Overview of the Test/Test Format:

0%: Russia Under the Old Regime
2% The Revolutionary Period 1914-1921
3%: Pre-War Stalinism
4%: The Second World War
1%: Postwar Stalinism
0%: The Khrushchev Years
0%: The Brezhnev Years
0%: Reform and Collapse

How I Studied for this Exam:

The way that I studied for this exam is the way I studied for a large portion of my exams; through study.com. I continue to recommend this site because of the way that it operates. It has teachers teach short video lessons that are on average 8-10 minutes, after each of them you take a short 5-8 question quiz to see if you grasped the material. These video lessons are divided into chapters, which all have a short test towards the end of them. After you complete all of the chapters you take a practice exam, which tells you if you are likely to pass or fail your actual exam. The one downside to this is that it costs $100 per month to use. But I assure you is well worth it.

Now this exam is not fully covered by study.com; so in addition to using this website I also watched many documentaries from all over the internet, as well as documentaries from the library. The Library is a great source for any type of knowledge you want. Including audio books that you can listen to while you're driving in the car and help you understand better. I would strongly recommend using the library.

The Mason Difficulty Rating:
4 out of 10 (relatively easy)

My Personal Review on the Test:

Next to the Vietnam War DSST this was my second favorite. It is also so interesting because it affected the world not long ago at all. This test as a whole requires a lot of specific knowledge; which is easily attained all over the internet with documentaries and books. The library is again a great location for this topic. I would strongly recommend this topic, because it is actually really interesting to see how evil and twisted it was in the Soviet Union.

Overview on Steps to Pass Exam

List of Steps Needed to Take to Complete College in a year:

1. **Stay positive**- Never forget to ignore people telling you no. Absolutely anybody can do this, and do it with ease. Believe in yourself, trust your passing rate and keep your life moving.

2. **Find a school that accepts the most amount of CLEP/DSST credits**- Spend a little time on the internet researching what school that would be best for you. I personally recommend online schools, my school was Southern New Hampshire University online. I strongly believe that online schools operate much better, and are much cheaper. But if you would like to be on campus, by all means, do that.

3. **Decide which degree you will achieve**- Once you have found the best possible school for the CLEP/DSST scenario, pick a major you would like or need to have your degree in. Do not go undeclared, or attempt to flip around your degrees unless you guarantee you won't lose progress.

4. **Map out which CLEPs/DSSTs you need for your degree**- Once you pick your program preference or have it narrowed down to a couple of options, figure out which CLEPs/DSSTs fit into the categories you need. Example: if you need a math course; and your college accepts the Precalculus CLEP, write out a checklist write out all of the CLEPs you need. Mark Precalculus in an "exams you have to take list."

5. **Begin taking tests**- you can either take them before you start college or at the same time as you take other classes. I personally did them at the same time;

however, at one point I took a 3-month break, in which I completed 24 of my credit hours with CLEPs/ DSSTs. It is much easier to complete when you are not currently attending classes. However, I succeeded while doing both as well as just focusing on CLEPs/DSSTs.

6. **Keep your momentum-** Don't give up half way through because it will be harder to come back from your hiatus. Stay focused, and keep your plan on the right path and try to stay consistent.

7. **Get your degree-** Once you finish all the CLEPs/DSSTs possible and take your last test, you must finish up your classes with your college. Once those are finished you are completely done. You have your degree and you can get to the next chapter in your life.

Made in the USA
Middletown, DE
16 August 2019